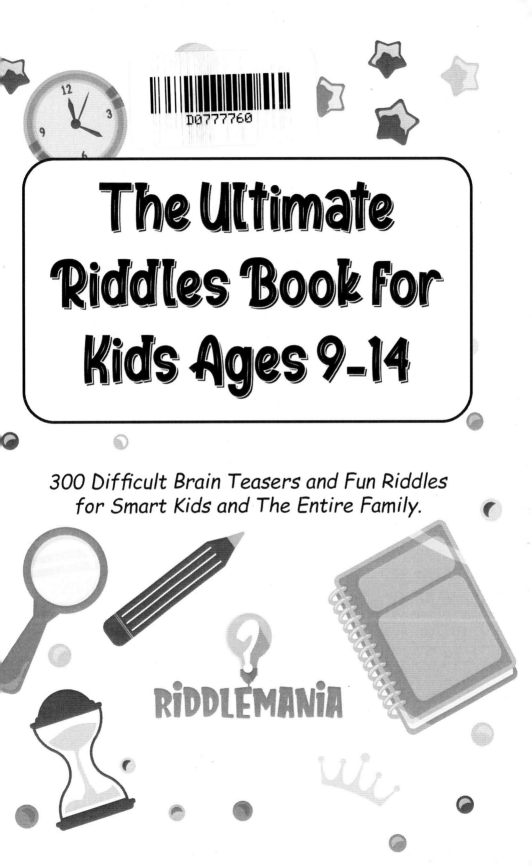

The Ultimate Riddles Book For Kids Ages 9-14

300 Difficult Brain Teasers and Fun Riddles
for Smart Kids and The Entire Family.

RIDDLEMANIA

Claim your 20 FREE jokes NOW!

Simply follow this link:
https://book.jokesnriddles.co.uk/

Or scan this QR code:

RIDDLEMANIA

Contents

Random Riddles

1. What day of the week is best for making eggs?

2. What letter knows the whole alphabet?

3. What kind of a shoe looks like you?

4. How can you share a secret if there's no one around?

5. What dessert do you get when you drop your groceries?

6. What band keeps coming back again and again?

7. What kind of insect brings you presents?

8. What has a hat it never wears?

9. How do you send a rocking chair to the moon?

1

10. Why can't bikes pedal themselves?

11. What gets buried twice?

12. What is your phone's favorite football team?

13. What's the most valuable symbol?

14. What direction does music come from?

15. Who is the deepest actor?

16. What sport has the most bugs?

17. What rainforest can you order just about anything from?

18. What kind of tree can you hold in your hand?

19. What is both tired and exhausting?

20. What kind of slide does your mom never want to see you on?

21. What do you get when someone wants to teach you about wood?

22. What kind of a key opens a banana?

23. What kind of flower doesn't have petals?

24. Earth and Mars are the only planets in the solar system that don't have what?

25. What is the only letter of the alphabet you can eat?

26. Why didn't the computer's facial recognition work?

27. How much does social media weigh?

28. What does macaroni and cheese watch for entertainment?

29. Why were the Eastern Europeans in a hurry?

30. What's the most common vowel in Canada?

31. What is the only letter of the alphabet you can drink?

32. How do chickens taste?

33. How do influencers use rafts?

34. What do you do after you tie a bow?

35. Who rules the sea?

36. What passes gas without having to be excused?

37. Who do you go see when you want to get stronger?

38. What has a trunk and leaves but is not a tree?

39. What kind of music will never die?

40. What do you call orderly lines of ships?

41. What do you call a pig with three eyes?

42. What condiment is always added from behind?

43. What gift are you always receiving?

44. What day of the week should you get married on?

45. How much does a deer cost?

46. Which two presidents belong in the Rose Garden?

47. What goes up but never comes down?

48. If you have type A blood when you go into the blood bank, but type S blood when you come out, what type do you actually have?

49. What kind of boat is cheaper than all the rest?

50. What do you get when you heat up a tiny glass of water quickly?

51. What kind of test does a balloon hate?

52. What kind of TV show is a squeaky-clean musical?

53. What is the calmest vegetable?

54. How did the golfer get to the golf course?

55. Why did George, Tom, Abe, Alex, Andrew, and Ben need to be saved?

56. What part of the house hurts the most?

57. What kind of fish takes your bait?

58. What position did the musician play in baseball?

59. George Washington told the truth about cutting down the cherry tree, but where did he lie?

60. What hand-me-down does every person get from their parents?

61. Which side of a zebra has the most stripes?

62. Why don't bears wear shoes?

63. How did the mouse die?

64. What color is the wind?

65. Why did the frog car disappear?

66. How can you avoid your coffin?

67. What's under there?

68. What's a pillow's favorite video game?

69. What insect is the most religious?

70. What kind of board can you crumple?

71. What separates Australia from the Pacific Ocean?

72. What animal is the worst driver?

73. Where do you see yourself in five years?

74. What's a clay pot made with?

75. What kind of mine is the busiest during Valentine's Day?

76. Whom do ghosts date?

77. What kind of fish never share?

78. What herb is there always more of?

79. What's the worst icebreaker to go down in history?

80. What was the whaler doing in the waiting room?

81. What do penguins use to hold their houses together?

82. What goes up when rain comes down?

83. What kind of sandwiches replace regular sandwiches?

84. What has windows you can't see out of?

85. Where can you find a football player at a wedding?

86. What shape is the loudest?

87. Who gave birth to the Egyptians?

88. What kind of flower do you always have under your nose?

89. What's a cow's favorite thing from McDonald's?

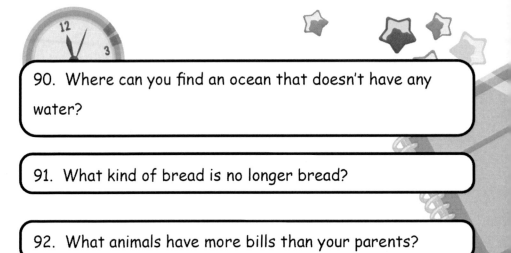

90. Where can you find an ocean that doesn't have any water?

91. What kind of bread is no longer bread?

92. What animals have more bills than your parents?

93. What does cheese say when you take its picture?

94. What three-letter word can you put every other letter into?

95. What word is just as fast forward as it is backward?

96. What part of every room has corn in it?

97. What kind of room can you eat?

98. What kind of shipping container always has a rat in it, even when it's empty?

99. What can you put in the middle of a desert to make everyone want it?

100. Why do safe drivers use pencils?

101. What's orange and sounds like a parrot?

102. What has one eye and many ears but can't hear or see?

103. What kind of comb do you never want to put in your hair?

104. What month has its own parade?

105. What is the best day to move forward?

106. Where do you go to learn how to wear armor and ride horses?

107. What five-letter word can you add two letters to, and make it shorter?

108. What kind of leader is only 12 inches tall?

109. What word has all the letters in it?

110. What does a can opener become when it no longer works?

111. What can you use to write that always has ink in it?

112. What is slippery forwards but dreamy backwards?

113. What's at the end of a rainbow?

114. What makes dinos sore?

115. How do you navigate through space?

116. What kind of cookies do you not want to eat?

117. How did the old lady catch a fish without a pole?

118. What fruit can you create by combining two types of trees?

119. What's frightening with a car inside of it?

120. What word has the most Cs in it?

121. I'm in space but I'm not a planet, asteroid, or star. I can be high and I can be low. You can find me in a deck of cards. What am I?

What Am I?

122. I help cereal killers and I'm what you get when you combine a bee with an owl. What am I?

123. I lose my head every day but get it back every night. What am I?

124. I have a roof but no floor. What am I?

125. You can find everything in the known universe inside of me, but I can be held in your hands. Sometimes I die, but I never really live. What am I?

126. I am covered in hair but I'm not a mammal. What am I?

127. I have ten fingers but no toes. What am I?

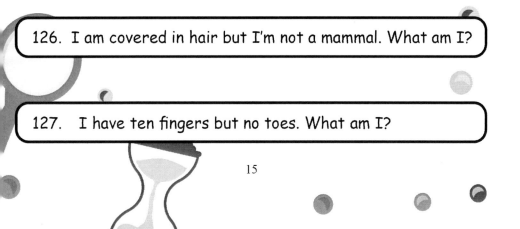

128. I can charge, but I don't need a power cord. I have horns, but they don't honk. You can drive me, but I don't have wheels. What am I?

129. I'm a type of plant, but I don't need water. I can hurt people, but I'm not poisonous. I'm almost always found on the ground when you least expect it. (Sorry about your nose.) What am I?

130. I have a tongue, but I don't lick. I can walk but not by myself. I'm almost never alone. What am I?

131. I'm half sand, but I'm not sandy. I'm more edible than I am magic. I don't ride brooms, but brooms sweep up my mess. What am I?

132. I rise every day and go across the sky. Sometimes I'm out at night, but never without people. What am I?

133. Sometimes I'm a blanket. Sometimes I'm a ball. I can turn into a person or into water. I'm a million different things but I'm always cold. What am I?

134. I'm not a boat but I float. I'm full of water but I never sink. You won't find me in oceans, lakes, or rivers. I can weigh a million pounds, but you won't find me on the ground. I reign in the sky. What am I?

135. I'm a star, but I'm not in the sky. I'm underwater, but I'm not a fish. What am I?

136. I always make my attackers cry, even though they cut me to pieces. What am I?

137. I share a name with a person and come around once a year for Christmas, but I am not Santa. What am I?

17

138. Sometimes I crawl, sometimes I fly. You can get stuck in me, which is usually when I start to honk. What am I?

139. I usually come out in the dark, but when I'm out, it's not dark. What am I?

140. Everyone uses me to keep warm. I have a match, but I don't start fires. I cover you and you cover me. What am I?

141. I have legs but I can't walk. I have arms but I can't hug. I have a back but no spine and a seat, but I can't sit. What am I?

142. I have a back and a spine to protect my insides, but my insides are open to anyone. What am I?

143. I live underground and almost never move, but when I do, you feel it and that's my fault. What am I?

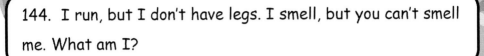

144. I run, but I don't have legs. I smell, but you can't smell me. What am I?

145. You can find me underground and I'm full of carrots, but you can't eat me. What am I?

146. If you remove the bee, I'm cold air. Without the sea, I'm muscle. Take away my first part and I'm ancient. I can be read, but usually I'm sung. What am I?

147. You can reboot me, but I'm not electronic. What am I?

148. You use me to unlock but I'm not a key. But without keys, I don't exist. What am I?

149. I'm a bank and sometimes I make deposits, but I don't have any money. I do have plenty of flow. What am I?

150. My keys can make a jingle but they won't open doors. I have more than two legs, but almost never four. What am I?

151. I'm a kid, but I don't go to school. I'm not the greatest of all time, but I could be. What am I?

152. I can't speak, but I am loud. I can say hello, but I don't have hands. I always crash, but I never get hurt. I have many ups and downs. What am I?

153. I open and close but I don't have a lid. You can see me and hear me, but you can never taste me. I'm something you can feel, but I can't be touched. I'm long but cannot be measured in inches. I'm really light. What am I?

154. I have rabbit ears but I don't hop. Sometimes I'm black and white, but I can have more colors. I have lots of power but I'm mostly forgotten. Most of your grandparents used to watch me. What am I?

155. I have a toilet, a shower, and a sink but I'm not a bathroom. What am I?

156. I'm a tank but I never go to war, yet I'm always bloody. What am I?

157. I have eyes but I can't see. My skin is rough and I am hard. But you usually encounter me when I'm soft. What am I?

158. I break easily but even the strongest man can't break me by squeezing with one hand. You must break me to use me. What am I?

159. I have roads but you can't drive on them. I have buildings but you can't go in. I have a key that doesn't open anything. What am I?

160. I'm always up to something when something is going down. I don't have a problem with you looking at me for a long time. What am I?

161. When I'm working properly, I break, and when I break, I work. But when I'm broken, I don't work.
What am I?

162. I can fly but I don't have wings. I can stand still, even though I never stop. Some have too much of me, but most not enough. What am I?

163. I run but I don't have feet. If I have multiple feet, I'm usually still. What am I?

164. You can count on me, but only up to a certain point. I have a good grasp on things and am something to behold. I'm very touchy. What am I?

165. Despite my name, I'm actually very hot. I can be a plant or mixed up in a pot. What am I?

166.   I can wake you up, but I don't make a sound. Most people have used me, but you've never seen me. I can be strong, and I can be weak. You can't feel me unless I'm inside you. What am I?

167. I have multiple stitches, but I've never been to the hospital. I've been hit thousands of times, but it doesn't hurt. I get out a lot and sometimes feel safe. Some would say I'm quite the catch. What am I?

168. I can be open or closed, but I'm not a door. I can be empty, and I can be full. I can be twisted and I can be dirty. Everyone has one, but not everyone uses it.
What am I?

169. I'm where you go to curl up and die. But when you leave, you feel more alive. What am I?

170. I'm not heavy and I'm not hot, but you can only hold me for a short amount of time. What am I?

171. I go to school but not to learn. I'm not an adult.
What am I?

172. I have a head and I have a tail. I don't have a body.
I can do flips. What am I?

173. I snap without breaking and can capture moments. What am I?

174. I'm a pear but I'm not a fruit. Sometimes you can find me on powerlines, but usually, I'm on the ground. What am I?

175. I'm a form of shade but I make things bright. What am I?

176. What kind of rapper doesn't rhyme?

177. I have appeal but sometimes can make people slip up. What am I?

178. What I am and what I do are the same, depending on where you put the E. You can find me in the grass, in the water, or in a tree. What am I?

179. I never move, but I'm associated with moving. What am I?

180. I can be a letter, a person, or a quality. What am I?

181. You can roll me but I'm not round. I'm a plate but you can't eat off me. I can be found indoors but seen outside. What am I?

182. I have five rings and zero fingers. I'm not a planet, but I represent one. What am I?

183. I'm a little horse but I'm not a pony. I have two legs, but they are not what is running. What am I?

184. You can slice me while driving but I'm not food. I start with a T, and I'm a hit at the club. What am I?

185. You can push me or move me to the side. I'm not in the way, but I clear a path. What am I?

186. You walk on me but I'm not the ground or the floor. Other people can step on me, but you can't. What am I?

187. You can cut me but I don't bleed. I have many hearts and I'm kind of a big deal. What am I?

188. I need to be consoled but I'm not sad. I don't have control of myself, but I do have control. Let's play. What am I?

189. I'm under the weather but I'm not sick. I'm over your head but you get me. What am I?

190. I'm made to be broken and everyone wants a piece of me. You tie me up and hit me with a stick, even though inside I'm really sweet. What am I?

191. I light up when you walk into a room. I can be a good idea but sometimes I'm a little dim. What am I?

192. I have two legs, but I can't walk. I have a waist but no insides. My bottom is on top, and I always have a fly. What am I?

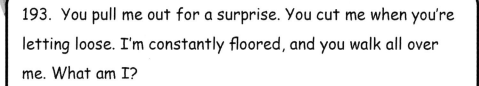

193. You pull me out for a surprise. You cut me when you're letting loose. I'm constantly floored, and you walk all over me. What am I?

194. You can roll me up, but you can't roll me down. I have two lids that don't stay closed. You use me every day. What am I?

195. I can be a bit of a hothead, but only if you strike me. What am I?

196. I start with one cup, but I can fit much more inside. I have one board, but I'm made from more wood than that. What am I?

197. I'm known to be wise because I'm always asking, "Who?" I actually have a bird brain. What am I?

198. I don't need scissors to cut but you can cut me with scissors. Sometimes I have a lot to say and other times I am at a loss for words. You can use me to do the right thing. What am I?

199. I'm not a vegetable or a nut. I have a shell, but I'm not found in the ocean. Sometimes I'm crunchy, and sometimes I spread. What am I?

200. I'm a big hit in the park, but even bigger out of it. I always end up back at home and I don't get out. What am I?

201. You put me on your ears and your nose. I'm not sunscreen, but I help protect you from the sun. What am I?

202. I'm a belt that you wear but not to hold up your pants. I'm not fashionable but I'm very important. What am I?

What Am I?

203. I am the first King to lead in America. Who am I?

204. We proved gravity wrong. Who are we?

205. People associate me with the word "fast" but I am a slow and peaceful person. My last name ends with "D" but it's spelled "hi". You might not have any idea, if you're not from India. Who am I?

206. I sneak into bedrooms and steal body parts from children, yet people love me. I love to make you smile, even if it's missing pieces. Who am I?

207. I'm not a candy bar, I'm not a baby, and I'm not a woman. My name might make you think differently, but wait till you see me swing a bat. Who am I?

208. My name is not bruise, despite how it sounds. But I know kung fu, and I can bruise people - but only when they won't LEEave me alone. Who am I?

209. I'm round and smooth on top and big and bulky. I'm not a boulder, but you can roll my film. Who am I?

210. No matter where you are, I'm always across. Who am I?

211. My brain is not dough, it's actually quite smart. But you can't play with me, because I died a long time ago. Who am I?

212. I'm not a place of worship on a raised plot of land. I led men in battle. Who am I?

213. My life is in ruins, but I dig it. Who am I?

214. I must have a lot of patience to do my job, but it doesn't matter how patient I am. Who am I?

215. I drive away all my customers but they still pay me. Who am I?

216. I'm a web developer who doesn't type. I crawl but not online. Who am I?

217. I always let people use my things, just like my name. Who am I?

218. I live in front of your door. Who am I?

219. I really need my space. Who am I?

220. You wait for me, not the other way around. You only see me when you're hungry. Who am I?

221. When I fly low, I make you act like me. Who am I?

222. I run into people for a living. Who am I?

223. I have more dates than the average girl. Who am I?

What is it?

224. What kind of ticket costs a lot of money, but doesn't get you into a show?

225. You can find this in any house, but usually they aren't shared. You can take as many as you want. There's always another. When you take one, you always leave something behind. What is it?

226. Every student uses this paper but they never write on it. What is it?

227. What has a bed but never sleeps?

228. What can you catch without hands?

229. What piece of clothing do you soak in hot water, and then drink the water?

230. What kind of shark fixes you after they bite you?

231. What is faster than a second?

232. What type of ham would make the best president?'

233. What living thing has the quietest bark?

234. What runs but stays in one place?

235. What kind of chip takes the most bites?

236. What kind of dog can you eat?

237. What country is made of stone?

238. What's sticky but you can't stick to it?

239. It's something you saw in the forest, but not with your eyes. What is it?

240. What has a beat and rhymes with art?

241. What's tough to crack and sounds like a sneeze?

242. What has three feet but no legs?

243. What son doesn't have a father?

244. What can only be missed when it's present?

245. What kind of plant is a pilgrim's favorite?

246. What kind of bird can you find at a construction site?

247. What has four wheels and flies?

248. What makes up everything?

249. What has teeth but doesn't bite?

250. What kind of nail doesn't get hammered?

251. What becomes bigger, the more you take away from it?

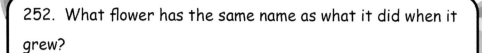

252. What flower has the same name as what it did when it grew?

253. What kind of photo can you breathe?

254. What animal is the most dishonest?

255. What kind of steam does a person who loves taking pictures of themselves need?

256. You can check me out but, if you do it for too long, you get fined. What am I?

257. What does the USA use to connect?

258. What comes in a can and rhymes with anything?

259. What animal is also a really cool letter?

260. What animal is next to long in the dictionary?

261. What can you blow up without dynamite?

262. What do fish get hooked on?

263. No matter how fast you use it, it always comes in #2. What is it?

264. What goes in diapers?

265. What kind of boxer always goes down?

266. What kind of app can you touch with your fingers but not on your phone?

267. What kind of float can you bring to a parade, but you won't see it in the parade?

268. What kind of chalk can you eat?

269. The eyes have it. The 'i's have it. But the ayes do not. What is it?

270. What kind of bug is the most musical?

271. What insect is created from throwing dairy across the room?

272. Which metal is the most attractive?

273. What's white and gets into every recipe?

274. What always gets the last word?

275. What has four legs and is good for eating?

276. What do you call a drink without ice?

277. What rhymes with goop that you always put in a bowl?

278. What kind of duck never flies south for the winter?

279. What kind of drums do all musicians have?

280. What kind of bar has the most room?

281. What kind of cow makes Swiss cheese?

282. What is not a bear but is good at cooking?

283. What runs around your yard but doesn't have legs?

284. What kind of hole can't be filled but can fill you?

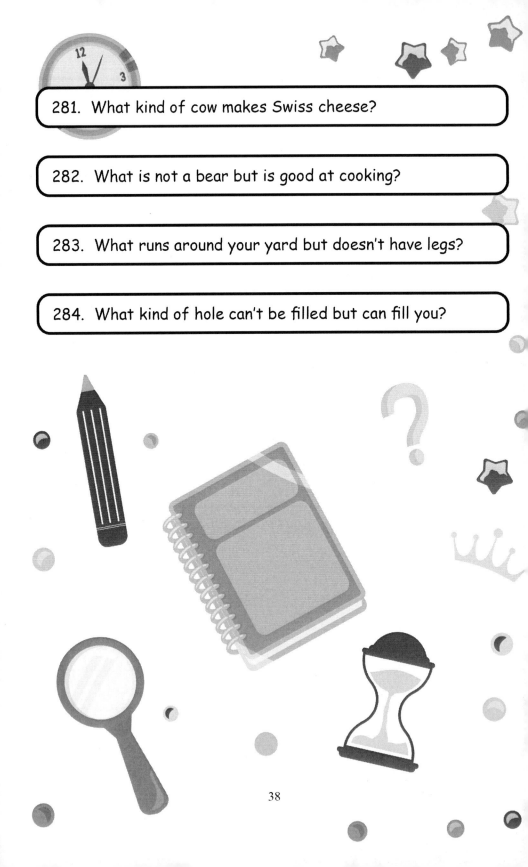

Silly Number Riddles

285. What number doesn't have square roots but is divisible by an axe.

286. What fruit is good at division?

287. What do you get when you add two minus signs?

288. What number is bad at golf?

289. Why are magazines good for doing your math homework?

290. What type of toilet paper never runs out?

291. Why did the math students refuse to split off into groups?

292. What is the biggest table in the world?

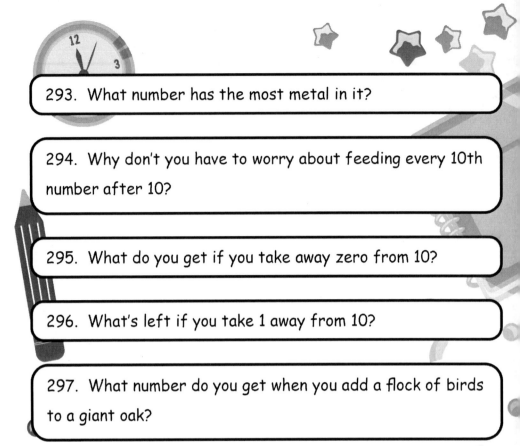

293. What number has the most metal in it?

294. Why don't you have to worry about feeding every 10th number after 10?

295. What do you get if you take away zero from 10?

296. What's left if you take 1 away from 10?

297. What number do you get when you add a flock of birds to a giant oak?

298. What is always on time?

299. What book is the saddest?

300. What number is the tastiest?

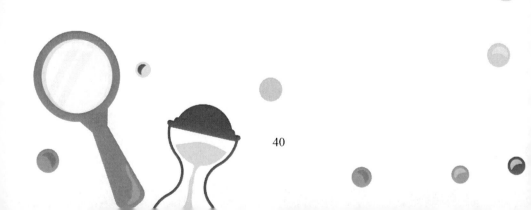

40

Answers

RANDOM RIDDLES

1. Fry-day.

2. U.

3. A horseshoe.

4. Tell-a-phone.

5. A milkshake.

6. A rubber band.

7. Aunts.

8. What has a hat it never wears.

9. Rock-it.

10. They're two-tired.

11. A berry bush.

12. The Chargers.

13. A check.

14. Kanye West.

15. Brad Pitt.

16. Cricket.

17. Amazon.

18. A palm tree.

19. A car.

20. A mudslide.

21. Board.

22. A monkey.

23. Baking flour.

24. U.

25. Pea.

26. It had a really poor memory.

27. An Instagram.

28. Cheesy YouTube (U-tube) videos.

29. They were Russian (rushing).

30. Eh.

31. Tea.

32. With their tongue.

33. As live streaming platforms.

34. Shoot an arrow.

35. Vik**ings**.

36. A pipe.

37. Gym.

38. An elephant on vacation.

39. Rock.

40. Row boats.

41. A piiig.

42. Ketchup.

43. The present.

44. Wed.

45. A buck.

46. George H.W. Bush and George W. Bush.

47. Your age.

48. Typ-O.

49. A sailboat.

50. Microwaves.

51. A pop quiz.

52. A soap opera.

53. Peas (peace).

54. With a driver.

55. They're on money (presidents).

56. The window pane.

57. A steel trout.

58. First bass.

59. In bed.

60. Genes.

61. The outside.

62. They have bear feet.

63. Its battery ran out (computer mouse).

64. Blew.

65. It was toad.

66. Cough suppressant.

67. Underwear (under where?).

68. Fortnite (fort night).

69. A praying mantis.

70. Cardboard.

71. The Great **Barrier** Reef.

72. A roadhog

73. A mirror.

74. Hands.

75. Be mine.

76. Their boo.

77. Shellfish.

78. Thyme.

79. The Titanic.

80. Waiting for a whale.

81. Igloo.

82. Umbrellas.

83. Subs.

84. A computer.

85. The reception.

86. The triangle (musical instrument).

87. Mummy.

88. Tulips (two lips).

89. Straw.

90. On a map.

91. Toast.

92. Ducks.

93. Nothing. Cheese can't talk.

ENGLISH WORD RIDDLES

94. Box.

95. Racecar.

96. Corner.

97. A mushroom.

98. A crate.

99. An S (dessert).

100. In case of an accident.

101. A carrot.

102. A corn field (one "i" plus ears of corn).

103. Honeycomb.

104. March.

105. March forth.

106. Knight School.

107. Short.

108. A ruler.

109. Mailbox.

110. A can't opener.

111. Thinking.

112. Peels (sleep).

113. W.

114. Asteroids.

115. You plan-it.

116. Computer cookies.

117. Internet (in her net).

118. Pineapple.

119. Scary.

120. Oceans (there are 7 seas).

121. Ace.

122. A bowl.

123. A pillow.

124. A mouth.

125. A cellphone (internet).

126. A barbershop.

127. Gloves.

128. A bull (cattle).

129. Faceplant.

130. A shoe.

131. A sandwich.

132. A plane.

133. Snow.

134. A cloud.

135. A starfish.

136. An onion.

137. (Christmas) Carol

138. Traffic.

139. A flashlight.

140. Socks.

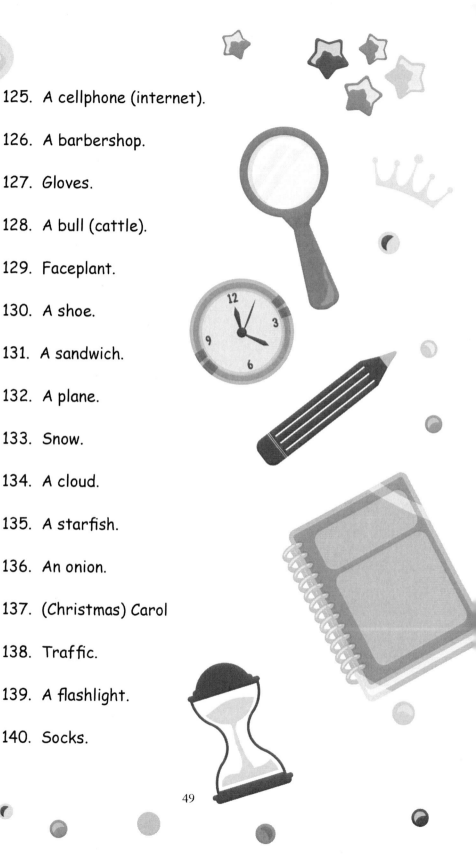

141. A chair.

142. A book.

143. Earthquake.

144. A nose.

145. A diamond.

146. ABCs

147. A foot.

148. A password.

149. A river bank.

150. A piano.

151. A baby goat.

152. A wave.

153. A movie.

154. An old-school TV.

155. A hardware store.

156. A tank of piranha.

157. A potato.

158. An egg.

159. A map.

160. Stairs.

161. Brakes.

162. Time.

163. Water.

164. Fingers.

165. Chili.

166. Caffeine.

167. A baseball.

168. Mind.

169. Hair salon.

170. Your breath.

171. A fish.

172. A coin.

173. A camera.

174. Shoes.

175. A lampshade.

176. A candy wrapper.

177. A banana.

178. A snake (sneak).

179. A house.

180. Character.

181. Car windows.

182. The Olympic logo.

183. Sick.

184. A golf ball (every golf ball starts on a tee!).

185. A broom.

186. Your feet.

187. A deck of cards.

188. A video game.

189. An umbrella.

190. A pinata.

191. A lightbulb.

192. Pants.

193. A rug.

194. Eyes.

195. A match.

196. A cupboard.

197. An owl.

198. Paper.

199. A peanut.

200. A home run.

201. Sunglasses.

202. A seatbelt.

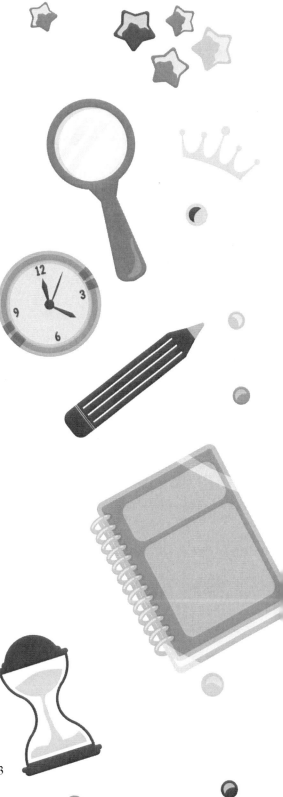

WHO AM I?

203. Martin Luther King Jr.

204. The Wright brothers.

205. Gandhi.

206. The Tooth Fairy.

207. Babe Ruth.

208. Bruce Lee.

209. Dwayne "The Rock" Johnson.

210. Jesus.

211. Plato.

212. Winston Churchill.

213. An archaeologist.

214. A doctor.

215. A driver.

216. A spider.

217. Sharon.

218. Matt.

219. An astronaut.

220. A waiter.

221. Duck.

222. A football player.

223. A calendar girl.

WHAT IS IT?

224. A speeding ticket.

225. A shower.

226. Toilet paper.

227. A river.

228. A cold.

229. A Tea Shirt

230. A nurse shark.

231. A first.

232. Alexander **Ham**ilton (he has a ton more than

Abra**ham** Lincoln)

233. A tree.

234. A dishwasher.

235. A computer chip (bytes).

236. A hotdog.

237. Iraq (a rock).

238. A stick.

239. Wood.

240. A rapper.

241. Cashew.

242. A yard.

243. The Sun.

244. Fog (mist).

245. Mayflower.

246. A crane.

247. A garbage truck.

248. Atoms.

249. A comb.

250. A toenail.

251. A hole.

252. Rose.

253. Photosynthesis.

254. The lion.

255. Selfie steam.

256. A library book.

257. USB.

258. Silly String.

259. A hippo (hip O).

260. A giraffe (neck's too long).

261. A balloon.

262. Worms.

263. A pencil.

264. Babies.

265. Boxer shorts.

266. Appetizers.

267. A root beer float.

268. Chocolate.

269. Little black dots.

270. The Beatles.

271. A butterfly.

272. Magnets.

273. Teeth.

274. A tombstone.

275. A table.

276. A drnk.

277. Soup.

278. A rubber duck.

279. Eardrums.

280. Space bar.

281. A holy cow.

282. A pan, duh.

283. A fence.

284. A donut hole.

SILLY NUMBER RIDDLES

285. Tree.

286. Bananas. They split.

287. An equal.

288. FOUR!

289. They have lots of ad space.

290. Multi-ply.

291. They were tired of all the division.

292. The multiplication table.

293. Tin.

294. Because twenty ate, thirty ate, forty ate, fifty

ate, sixty ate, seventy ate, eighty ate, and ninety ate.

295. 1.

296. 0.

297. Turdy tree.

298. A number.

299. A math book (it has lots of problems).

300. Pi.

Made in United States
North Haven, CT
07 July 2023

38654491R00037